Forex Strategies and Analysis for Day Traders

Profitable Investing with Currency Swaps, Hedges and Scalps for Both Beginning and Advanced Traders

An Introduction to Forex Trading

In 1971, foreign exchange currency rates switched from being fixed to floating and a new market opened up. The foreign exchange currency rates between two countries were now subject to the trading volume between them and their respective market dynamics. Since then, foreign trade and therefore foreign currency exchange trade has grown by leaps and bounds, reaching a turnover of more than US$3.2 Trillion in 2017 with a 71% increase since 2014. Foreign exchange trade became a new business opportunity which exploited the volatility of the exchange rates for profit.

The foreign exchange market is not only the biggest international trade market but is also the longest running, operating 24 hours a day except weekends. This makes it more sensitive to international events and therefore more respondent to market changes.

Learning forex trading is about learning how currencies are exchanged and it requires an in-depth knowledge of economic developments in the International markets, as well as domestic markets. The fundamentals are simple, but acquiring mastery over trading requires years of experience. Trading in this market is usually done on phone and nowadays, largely on the Internet. You can trade from anywhere in the world. All you need is an Internet connection, a decent capital investment and a willingness to learn. The cost of operation from the Internet is lower and also faster compared to traditional methods.

Learning Forex Trading

Trade in all forms is the buying and selling of goods. The principle on which it operates is 'buy low, sell high'. Forex trade is unique in the sense that there are no goods sold here, only currencies are swapped, one for the other. The principle of operation is the same though, 'Buy a currency as cheaply as possible and sell it when it improves in value' or 'sell a currency at a price and buy it back cheaper when its value falls'. The former kind of transaction is called a 'long position' while the latter is called the 'short position'.

There are many online brokerage companies that operate and provide the platform for trading currencies. Firstly, get familiar with the trading jargon. It takes a bit of time to learn, but once you get used to it, the operation is simple. The main thing is to understand the factors that affect the currency trading prices which are the markets, central bank policies and international trade. You could call the whole thing a very advanced form of betting, that is what forex trading is all about. You make choices based on informed guesses and hope for the best. The choices need to be made through a deep understanding of how a particular currency is going to respond to market dynamics.

You could and probably should start off with a practice account in which you do not actually trade but get used to the procedure of online trading. Read charts, make calculations and place virtual buy and sell orders before you start doing it with real money.

Another exercise you could do is follow and read the currency trade news in the financial papers. They give a daily quote and analysis of the exchange rates or you could get the live quotes online. Make your own virtual transactions based on the data. Make a table of your virtual profits and losses. Once you start beating the markets consistently and confidently on a regular basis, go ahead and make a real investment in the Forex markets.

Brokerage sites provide you with software programs and online tools for analysis and a forex account. You can start trading from the comfort of your home. Alternatively, you could take forex trade training which will give you the depth of knowledge and grasp of fundamental principles.

What you essentially do is trade between pairs of currencies which are listed in the order of their market value. Online trading is mostly 'direct exchange' of currencies which forms US$ 1.4 trillion of market share.

Currency Trading Basics

Currency trading happens for two reasons. The first, and the simplest reason is, a Mr. X from the United States wants to go for a holiday in Australia. But he fears that the US dollar might not be as easily accepted in Australia, because it has its own currency, the Australian Dollar. So to be able to buy gifts for the rest of his family, he decides that he'd better convert the USD to ASD to avoid any problems. Simple enough.

But another Mr. Y decides to buy Australian Dollar, not because he's looking for a sojourn on the Gold Coast, but because they are available at a rate which he believes will increase. Confused? Let me explain with the help of an example. Suppose today Mr Y can buy 3 ASD in exchange for 1 USD, and - just for a moment, assume that - he can sell them tomorrow for 2 USD, he's going to make a tidy little profit of $1 on what is widely known as the Foreign Exchange (Forex) Market. But why will the price of 3 ASD jump from 1 USD to 2 USD? Because of the fluctuations in the demand and supply of various currencies in the Forex market.

Foreign Currency Trading

First, let me explain why the price of the ASD is going up. The Forex market works on the old demand-supply model. This means that if the supply of one currency is less (in this case the ASD) and the demand for it is high, then the currency is going to command a higher price in the Forex trading market. Now Mr. Y must have done some very detailed research into the expected demand for the ASD before he came to the conclusion that since the demand will increase tomorrow, he can buy it today for a lower price and make a profit tomorrow. Roughly speaking, the Forex market too works like the stock market. Say you are holding the shares of Shell on the stock exchange, and if Shell finds some serious quantity of oil, then the price of the shares will shoot up and the current holders of shares of Shell will make a good profit. Similarly, if the price of a currency is expected to rise in the near future, one could buy the currency and then sell it at a higher price.

Now let us look at some basic terms used in currency trading and their meanings.

Bid/Ask:

In the Forex market, there are two prices. One is called the 'bid' price and the other is called the 'ask' price. For example, let's say the price of a EUR/USD (one Euro to US dollars) was 1.4161/65. Out of these two the 'bid' price is the lower one (1.4161) and is the dollar price that the person who wants to buy the Euro is quoting i.e. he is offering to buy 1 Euro in exchange for $1.4161. The second number (1.4165) is the price that the holder of the Euro is 'asking' i.e. the person who is holding the Euro is demanding 1.4165 dollars in exchange for the 1 Euro.

Pip:

A pip (price interest point) is the incremental move which one currency makes over the other. In the previous example, we took the EUR/USD to be 1.4161, if the bidder ups his bid to 1.4165 to match the asker's rate, then it is said that there was a move of 4 pips. If the currency prices are more disparate - like in the case of GBP/INR, (English Pound to Indian Rupee) if it moves up from 78.86 to 78.92 it is still a jump of 6 pips. Pips are calculated on the last two digits on the right of the decimal point.

Why Does the Demand for a Currency Increase/Decrease

Since the price of the currency is largely dependent on the demand for it, we need to understand what causes the shifts in the demand while learning currency trading. By knowing what causes of the changes in demand, we can make an informed decision on whether or not to buy the currency or sell the currency we have in hand. The factors which influence the demand are GDP, inflation and interest rates, trade agreements between the countries whose currency is being traded, budget plans, budget deficits, how the national stock market is doing and overall economic and political soundness of the country. For example, suppose the capital market of an emerging market like Brazil is doing rather well. And the nation is earning a substantial GDP and there are no political troubles whatsoever. In such a case, Brazil will be viewed as a potential target for multinationals to invest in. The Brazilian stock market will also come under the radar of foreign institutional investors. Hence, to invest in Brazil and Brazilian companies, one will need Brazilian currency. So the Brazilian currency will be in great demand. This drives the price of the Brazilian Real higher.

The currency market is a highly speculative market and one needs to do very detailed research before buying currency, in order to make a profit.

Types of Forex Transactions

There are many ways in which forex transactions can occur differing in volume and time of transaction. They are:

Swap:

The most common type of transaction that happens in forex markets, the swap is an exchange of currencies for a previously decided period of time followed by re-exchange by mutual agreement. These dealings do not happen by contracts. These transactions are most common in the market.

Spot:

As the name suggests, a spot transaction is an exchange of currencies done in the shortest time, usually 2 days and in cash. Interest rate is not applied in the transaction. It is a direct exchange transaction between two currencies. This is the second most common transaction after swap.

Forward:

A forward transaction is an agreement between a buyer and seller to purchase or sell a currency at a predestined future date by mutual agreement. The time period set may vary from days to months. These type of transactions reduce volatility risks.

Future:

This is another type of forward transaction but with a formal structure decided in the market. The buying and selling date is set for up to 3 months in the future and interest is inclusive in the price.

Option:

A derivative type of transaction is an option or FX option as it is called. In it, the buyer and the seller agree upon a future date for exchanging currency. Although the seller has a right to sell at that predestined date, he has no obligation to do so. This is a more flexible option than 'Forward' or 'Future' transactions.

Benefits of the Foreign Exchange Market

One advantage of the direct exchange Forex market is that liquidity is not a problem here. The market deals in liquid assets, that is currency. Make sure that after you have invested in the markets, you have a backup plan and some savings other than these investments. Do not place all your eggs in the same basket. I mean that metaphorically. It is a hectic form of trade and you need to be in touch with the market pulse all day.

The foreign exchange market is the (market)place where different currencies are traded for one another. As such, it is held to be the biggest financial market in the world, and one which is closest to the ideal of 'perfect competition' held by economists the world over. The traders in this market include currency speculators, banks, central banks, governments, multinational corporations, and other financial organizations.

The foreign exchange market is characterized by:

- Huge trading volumes
- 24 hour trading
- Geographical Diversity
- Liquidity
- Large variety and number of traders

The trading volumes of the forex market exceed billions of dollars and the market is open 24 hours a day because currency is traded all throughout the globe. This geographical diversity is the reason that a large variety of traders exist in the foreign exchange market today. Also adding to this diversity is the capability of different platforms such as Internet trading, (which we go into detail on later in this book) to create a diverse trader base in the market.

Of course, the fact that trade in this market consists of currency or foreign exchange is bound to create a very high amount of liquidity. The main feature of this market is that there is no central marketplace for the trade of foreign exchange. As such, the trade is carried out OTC or 'Over The Counter'.

Depending upon the kind of foreign exchange or currency instrument being traded, and the kind of trade being conducted, the prices vary. For example, the price for buying currency notes would be different from the price for buying checks. Similarly, a buy transaction exchange rate will differ from a sell transaction exchange rate.

There are a boundless number of currency pairs availibale, yet invariably the top 5 currencies which are traded in the foreign exchange market are:

United States Dollar (USD)

Eurozone Euro (EUR)

Japanese Yen (JPY)

British Pound Sterling (GBP)

Swiss Franc (CHF)

Currency rates are always expressed in terms of another, more popular or stable currency. For example, the exchange rate of the Indian Rupee is always expressed in comparison with the United States Dollar.

Factors Affecting Forex Currency Market Trade

Due to its particular features, foreign exchange rates and trade in the foreign exchange market are primarily the result of the demand and supply functions of currency. Other than this point of view, the Forex market is also affected by factors which can be broadly classified into:

Political Conditions:

Political conditions of a country can affect that country's currency rates. Growth and economic prosperity can positively affect the currency rates, while political upheaval like civil war can negatively affect the currency rates of that country.

Economic Factors:

Economic factors include things such as the budget deficit or surplus conditions of that country, the balance of trade situation, levels of inflation and the general trend of economic growth in that country.

Market Psycology:

Market psychology includes the susceptibility of the Forex market to rumors, perceptions of the market regarding the safety of a particular currency, and the definitive long term trends of a currency in the market.

All these factors contribute towards the currency rate of a particular country to rise or fall.

Components of Forex Currency Trading System

Forex Charts:

Forex charts, which might appear more like a series of crisscross lines for a layman, are actually comprehensive models of statistical information on countries, histories, national ties, and foreign and domestic events. These graphs can mark the difference between an intelligent speculator and ignorant investor. Forex charts help the investors to take the long view towards global trading and develop a comprehensive plan for investment.

Forex Rates:

Forex rates are the currency exchange rates which allow nations to exchange sums of money, for different purposes. If an individual wants to exchange money from one currency to another, he first needs to check the Forex rates. These rates are dependent on the politics and economic policies on local, regional, and international levels. The forex rates also provide an opportunity to gain tremendous profits by speculation.

Currency Speculation:

Currency speculators have always been a part of major economic controversies, and their effect on currency devaluations and national economies occurs regularly. However, they make a stabilizing influence on the market, despite the fact that they are considered to leave a negative impact on the currency market. Currency speculation is, sometimes also termed, as a kind of gambling, which often interferes with economic policy. There are also many contradictory views of economic scholars, who consider speculators as people who help the enforcement of international agreements, and anticipate the effects of basic economic laws. George Soros is multi-billionaire world famous currency speculator, who made a fortune by speculation.

Spot Transactions:

A spot transaction is a one- or two-day delivery transaction, which represents a direct exchange between two currencies and involves cash rather than a contract. The delivery time depends on the two currencies which are exchanged during the transaction, and the rate of interest is taken as its current value.

Forward Transactions:

In this kind of transaction, money transfer does not take place, until some agreed-upon future date decided by the buyer and seller. Suppose a firm wants to make payments to a foreign vendor for the imports, it can choose a day and make the payments on it. The exchange rate between two currencies is decided mutually by the broker and the buyer, and it remains same regardless of what the market rates are at the time of payment.

Forex currency trading is not conducted on a regulated exchange, because of which there are additional risks attached to it. The FX market was not always accessible to a regular trader, and as its access was limited to banks, hedge funds, major currency dealers and the high net-worth individual. Later, some smaller financial institutions and the growth of the Internet made forex available at a retail level. Before stepping into the forex arena, it is important for one to have an effective strategy to follow, which in turn will help gain benefits from this trading system.

How Forex Trading Works

The word Forex is an abbreviation of 'Foreign Exchange' or it is sometimes simply known as FX. This kind of market is a non-central, worldwide, over-the-counter market where currencies can be swapped and traded for corresponding prescribed values of trade. Forex trading essentially involves conversion of currencies at a certain specified exchange rate. The Forex market is one of the most complicated market as, lets face it, it consists of all currencies and indirectly all the national economies in the world.

Forex Trading Mechanism

The primary mechanism of Forex trade is as simple as a child's play. Every currency has a specified exchange rate which is chiefly used to convert it into a different currency. For example, a single US dollar can be exchanged into 0.702395168 Euro. This currency pair becomes the USD/EUR currency exchange pair. Though the actual transaction is in reference to a conversion, it is referred to as the purchase of the 'Euro'. In this pair of currency, the currency which has been used to purchase is known as the base currency, whereas the currency which has been converted into or has been purchased is known as the quote currency.

So how does this process actually materialize? As mentioned above this market is a worldwide market which is open throughout the day i.e. from 20:15 GMT (Greenwich Mean Time) on Sunday to 22:00 GMT of the immediate following Friday. Any person can invest into this market through a licensed broker, who charges commission for trades. Note that the legal systems and governing bodies such as the United States Securities and Exchange Commission often tend to impose certain governance and compliance on the trade processes, which people need to adhere to.

Making Money in the Forex Market

How to Make a Profit

So, how is profit made through the trades of the Forex? Every currency irrespective of the nation and the economy of the nation is influenced by two universal economic dissertations or corollaries:

- The currency value of any certain economy, tends to be influenced by the performance and growth of the economy, with respect the base currency.
- Similarly, the exports, development, disasters, internal banking, companies and other such countless features, which even include, wars and terror attacks, substantially affect the value of quote currency with respect to the base currency.

Now, both the aforementioned conditions tend to affect the values of both the base and quote currency. In this kind of situation you can make profit with the help of measures, namely:

- After you invest into the quote currency, you can wait for the quote currency's market value to raise, which increases your purchasing power to buy some other currency or re-buy your original base currency. So basically just by investing into well rising economy you are at position with higher currency value.
- The second type of measure which you can initiate is to wait till the value of your base currency drops down. Thus you shall be able to easily have a greater purchase value as you reconvert back into the base currency. In this measure, however you would not be able to convert your quote currency into any other currency than your base, as it may be either a situation of loss or a no-profit-no-loss situation.

Measurement of Profit or Loss

In this mechanism of Forex trade, one very big problem is that the Forex trade is characterized by the conversion of currencies, which is basically a barter. Hence there is no uniform way to measure profit or loss. In such a situation, the concept of PIP and BP is used.

PIP or Price Interest Point is the one unit change in the decimals of your base currency for example a change in USD $0.0001 (increase in cent) is known as 'one pip'. When one pip of the quote currency increases, you are at a profit of one pip. On the other hand if the base currency decreases by one pip, then you are still at an advantage.

The BP or the Base point is the per unit increase in non decimal value (dollars). For example, a change of $1.0000 in your base currency is the change in Base Point.

The formula to figure out the actual profit goes as:

PIP or BP / Current Exchange Rate = PIP or BP Value

The 'PIP' or 'BP' value is the currency actual currency value such as dollars and cents. The 'PIP' or 'BP' is expressed in percentage or units.

Now all these calculations and conversions are usually done by automated software, some of which in some cases also alert you about PIP changes.

How Safe is Forex Trading

The Forex market is known by many different names including the FX market, or simply the Foreign exchange market or even just currency trading. This market is a world wide, over the counter market, which is open of 6 days a week and is accessible world wide through a gigantic network of several different foreign exchange brokers, and intermediaries.

Point number one, Forex trading is not going to make you a millionaire with you just sitting back and relaxing, there is a lot of hard work involved in the process. Plus, you have to put in your own analysis and study, all with a great deal of carefulness.

Internationally any national currency which can be easily expressed and valued every day with the help of a parameter which is usually United States dollars. For example 1 Euro = 1.4021 U.S. Dollars or $1 equals 44.36 Rupees (INR). Since the United States dollar has been used as a measurement for investments, it is sometimes also known as the base currency. A person trading in Forex, basically invests say $5 into Euros of the same amount and waits. If the European union performs well, economically, then the value of invested Euros, appreciates, upon which the trader can reconvert the Euros into dollars which would now have appreciated to about say $7. As a trader you should be well versed with this mechanism and also have the Forex trading tips on your fingertips.

You can register with a broker who deals in Forex so as to make legal and secure trades in the market. Make sure that you register yourself with a broker who has an authorization to solicit your trades in the market. Also make sure to check his authorization, disclosures and the registration with the authorities, to ensure safety in Forex trading. Safe investment however is not restricted to just having a good broker.

So, is Forex trading safe? Well, to be really good at Forex trading and mitigate your risks, you also need to develop some good Forex trading strategies.

One of the best things that you can do is pair up economies. That is pair up United States Dollar with the Euro or the USD with the Yen. Monitor the two economies closely, and make an analysis of their demand and supply. Before investing make sure you track the rates of exchange between the two economies. This will give you good graph sense and anticipation judgment regarding the graphs of the currencies. The key to success is to purchase at a very ow expense and sell at a good rate. To know when to sell a particular currency and when to purchase one you will have to start learning statistical analysis of economies and also their demand and supply. There are some Forex trading techniques where the trades are done on sheer mathematical barrier breaks. That is if a particular currency breaks a certain barrier or exceeds certain value, then the trader sells the currency immediately. This strategy is often known as scalping. Another strategy is known as arbitrage trading where in the buy and sell action is almost simultaneous.

To keep your knowledge updated and senses alert you can use Forex signal providers which will alert you about the different changes in the world economies. The best way to cut your risk is to make sure that you remain alert and on your toes all the time. Remember, the market is not the same every day.

How to Trade in the Global Foreign Exchange Market

Foreign exchange trading or forex trading, is an interesting and profitable pursuit. If you strip the whole thing down to the bare essentials, it is just an exchange of a pair of currencies, one at a time. The maxim that applies to all profitable transactions applies here too, 'buy low, sell high'. Only the difference is that you do not buy or sell any goods in this trade. It's a barter system of currency, in which you exchange currency of one type for another with the intention of profiting from the transaction sooner or later. You buy a currency that you think will appreciate in value and you sell it when it does. Here 'buying a currency', means exchanging it for another type.

To master foreign exchange trade, like any other subject, you must find the best Forex training program and master its fundamentals. The fundamental thing that you need to understand is how the exchange rates are affected by global market developments. When you focus on two currencies, that you are exchanging, you need to monitor the import-export trends between those two countries and the liquidity in both the markets. You also need to monitor the global effects on the two currencies. If you are a beginner in this field, here are some tips from acclaimed masters of foreign trade:

Beware of Cheats

Just like every professional field, Forex trading has its share of cheats and con artists who are out there to dupe honest people. Always be suspicious of Forex brokerage companies that promise gargantuan profits with zero risk. They are surely con men, as every experienced Forex trader will tell you, big profits always come, after big risks are taken. Also be wary of brokerage companies that promise investing your money in the interbank market as it's not very transparent in its dealings. Make a thorough background check and verify the registration of the trading company before you set up your account with them.

Stay Connected with The Old Boys

If you want to be master of any trade, you have to learn from the masters. Get to know and stay in touch with experienced traders from the field. They have been there and done that. Learn from them as much as you can.

Do Your Homework

Stay connected with the latest happenings in the Forex market but don't get lost in data. Analyze and understand the cause and effect cycle in the forex market. Get an in depth knowledge of how the currency market is regulated and what factors affect its functioning. Understand why the numbers rise and fall and what causes exchange rate fluctuations. If you get your fundamental theory of Forex trading right and stick to the basics, things will more often turn out right.

Know Both Sides

When you are trading between two currencies, study them well. That is, follow developments on both sides and not just the high value side.

Too Many Cooks. . .

If you are giving your trading account over to a broker and he is going to operate for you, then let him! Let the man do his job, you may inquire, but do not meddle too much. If you are confident of trading alone, then make your own decisions after giving your ear to all.

Think Long Term

It's always the best policy to think long term when you are trading and it's also the mark of a good trader. Do not go for short term profits when your judgment tells you that things in long term will be better. Stick to your decisions and go for the kill, when you see a winner, and do not hesitate to sell out of a trade when you realize your mistake, out of stubbornness or hardheadedness.

It's All About Timing

Remember that it's all about timing, when it comes to trading. New developments in the market always start after the morning news is out, as credit policy changes by central banks and world business news influences the choices of investors world over. It is advisable that you avoid trading off peak hours. You do not need to trade 24x5. Fix your amount of working hours and get used to handling stress.

Keep it Simple

Keep your procedure simple and remember, you cannot control all the variables. So things are bound to go wrong in spite of all your preparation as the market is very fickle and driven by speculation. So be ready to brave the rough weather and steady your ship in the storm. Forex trading or any kind of business is not for the weak of heart!

How Does Currency Devaluation Work

Currency devaluation is lowering the value of a currency. The value of a devalued currency is low particularly to the other nations, because foreigners can now buy more goods in the same amount of money.

There are two ways in which a currency can be devalued.

1. Floating Exchange Rate System

Under the Floating Exchange System, the market forces devalues or revalues a currency, depending on the currency's demand and supply. If a currency's demand increases with respect to its supply, its value will increase and if a currency's demand falls with respect to its supply, it's value will fall.

2. Fixed Exchange Rate System

Under Fixed Exchange Rate System, a currency is devalued intentionally by the policy makers under the influence of the market pressures.

An economy can devalue its currency by printing more currency notes or by devaluing the currency under the Fixed Exchange Rate system. An economy can change its money supply by printing more notes and creating electronic bank credit and then it is added to the economy. Also the demand for a currency can increase significantly, if foreign countries demand their currencies for their local transactions. Similarly, if a currency's demand falls down, then it's currency faces devaluation. In times, when a currency's demand has lowered, a country devalues its own currency to attract other countries demand. As the currency is devalued, a foreign country will be able to buy more goods with the same amount of money. Therefore, tourists and importers will be willing to deal with countries which have devalued its currencies to gain profit margin.

Example: A lot of countries like China, Sri Lanka and Thailand have devalued their currency in the past to increase their exports and to increase tourism. Devaluing their currency made their exports cheap for the importers and also the tourism would increase as it will now be more affordable for travelers.

Implications of Devaluation

1. Exports Favored

In devaluation, Domestic currency becomes cheaper than the other countries. This enables the foreigners to spend less money and get the same goods or get more goods at the same price.

2. Discourage Imports

In devaluation, imports become expensive as a domestic country will end up paying more money for the same quantity. This will discourage the importer to import more goods. Its effect can be bad and good both depending on the country's trade deficit and its self-sufficiency.

3. Aggregate demand is boosted

As imports are discouraged, people will start to buy more of the domestic goods. This will in turn increase the aggregate demand of the domestic goods in an economy.

4. Inflation

As the demand for domestic goods starts increasing, the demand for the domestic goods might outgrow the supply of the domestic goods, which will lead to inflation.

5. Domino Effect

If one nation has devalued its currency, other neighboring nations can take it as a threat; as foreigners will be more attracted to an economy which has devalued its currency. Looking at this scenario the other countries can also devalue its currency.

Advantages of Currency Devaluation

1. Increasing Exports

Devalued currency makes an economy's exports more favorable. This is because their currency has become cheaper than other countries, increasing the demand from the importers.

2. Domestic Prices Remain the Same

This is one major advantage that a country can attain increasing foreign exchange reserves without affecting the domestic value of their currency, per se. The major impact of this will be felt by those who deal with imports and exports for business and arbitragers who try to profit from small variations in different currencies. Though, devaluation in the long run does have ill-economic effects; like inflation.

3. Growth Because of Increased Money Supply

Devaluation will lead to an increased money supply in an economy, which in turn will increase aggregate consumption, demand, saving and investment. All these increments will lead to some amount of growth in an economy.

4. Balance Trade Deficits

Devaluation can be a way in which a country can discourage imports (if a country's imports are more than their exports) and balance the trade deficits by making imports more expensive.

5. Fight Unemployment

Reduced imports lead to increase in the demand for domestic goods. This increases the domestic supply of goods in an economy and which in turn increases economic activities that require more manpower; leading to increasing employment rates and reducing unemployment rates.

Disadvantages of Currency Devaluation

1. Imports Become Expensive

If a major part of an economy is dependent on imports then, devaluation can lead to major economic losses.

2. Inflation

Increased money supply, increased domestic demand can increase the prices of the domestic goods, leading to inflation.

3. Hyper-stagflation

This occurs in a situation where a currency is devalued and it results into inflation accompanied with a high unemployment rate. This is a bad situation, as the rising prices lead to further unemployment and the current wages are not sufficient to keep the employed in par with the current prices.

4. Creditworthiness Maybe Threatened

Devaluation of a currency is a sign of economic weakness, which can hamper the creditworthiness of an economy in the global market; Making it very unreliable.

5. Capital Flight

Devaluation of a currency makes the investors very skeptical about the economy's future prospects. Therefore, they would look at withdrawing their investments from Foreign Institutional Investments and Foreign Direct Investments, leading to a situation of capital flight.

Dollar Devaluation

The U.S Dollar is said to have devalued over the period from 2002 to 2009. In 2002, the U.S dollar was valued against Euro as 1 Euro=$0.86. In 2009, this ratio become 1 Euro=$1.41. A resulting effect is said to be that the number of Americans traveling to Europe have reduced and the number of European travelers traveling to America had increased during that period. Also the number of American goods bought by the Europeans have increased and the number of European goods bought by the Americans have reduced considerably.

Devaluation of a currency is definitely not a good economic indicator. A country chooses to devalue its currency only when it does not find any other option to revive and stimulate the economy again. History says that devaluation of a currency can lead massive economic set back. The policy makers need to be very cautious and sensitive while dealing with economic problems under such circumstances.

Hedging Currency Risk

Over the past couple of years, volatility in the currency-exchange markets has made life tough for everyone who's involved with foreign currencies. Any executive or entrepreneur dealing with foreign currencies should know about hedging currency risks since it exposes a business to various new risks like exchange risks, interest rate risks, foreign exchange valuation exposure, etc. To counteract all these foreign exchange related risks, one must learn all about them.

Hedging Currency Risks

Hedging is the act of reducing or negating the risks that arise out of changes in the prices of one currency against another. In simpler words, if you had a certain amount payable in dollars in two months' time and had planned accordingly for it, only to find out that the dollar has appreciated with respect to your home currency, you'd be shelling out much more when the payable actually became due. The strategies that help in countering this risk of unexpected increase in payables and decrease in receivables come under the 'hedging currency risks' purview.

Note: There are three types of foreign currency risks, namely transactional risk (deals with changes in foreign currency exchange prices and their impact on a firm's cash transactions), translation risk (assesses the effect of changes in exchange rate on the financial condition of a company) and economic risk (measures the impact of exchange price changes on a firm's cash flow).

Options for Hedging Currency Risks

There are many ways to hedge foreign currency risks. You can use any of these foreign currency hedging methods to hedge foreign exchange risks and also for other risks, like for hedging interest rate risks.

Internal Hedging Strategies

Internal tactics like leading and lagging can ensure that you utilize the exchange rate movements to ensure that you always pay less and earn more. That is, when you can lead payments (pay them in advance) when you expect the home currency to depreciate with respect to the foreign currency. Similarly, netting the payments and receipts that are in the same foreign currency will also help reduce the exposure.

Forward Transactions

Hedging currency risks with forward transactions is a relatively easy to implement hedging strategy. In this, the currency payment or receipt is locked in at a particular exchange rate for a pre-specified rate in the future, irrespective of what the actual market exchange rate at that time is. The idea behind forward contracts is that as the exchange rate is locked on both sides, both, the creditor and the lender do not have to worry about fluctuations in the income and expenditure respectively.

Currency Futures

Currency futures are the same as forward contracts and are just for locking in an exchange rate for a pre-set date of the transaction in the future. The advantage that currency futures have over currency forwards is that as these are exchange traded, counter-party risk is eliminated. It also helps that currency futures are more transparent in their pricing and are more easily available to all market participants.

Currency Swaps

These exchange rate transactions are real-time transactions where one thing is just exchanged for another. These swaps can also be used for hedging interest rate risks where two parties can exchange their fixed and floating interest rate obligations with each other.

Currency Options

Currency options are financial instruments that give the owner the right but not the obligation to buy or sell a specific foreign currency at a predetermined exchange rate. While a call option gives the holder the right to buy the currency at an agreed price, a put option gives him the right to sell it at an agreed price, irrespective of an unfavorable market price for the same.

These were some of the traditional methods for hedging currency risks. Here are some of the newer strategies to achieve the same, that some companies like the UBS have brought forward for their customers.

Cancellable Forward

Some companies allow for cancellable forwards which are instruments that allow a regular currency cash flow to be hedged on a monthly rolling basis. The instrument requires no payment of premiums and gives better rates than those in the forward markets, but on the downside, the cash flows are not guaranteed and are always less favorable than the spot rates.

Range Reset Forward

This is an instrument based on market expectations and is perfect for you, if you think that the exchange rates between two currencies are going to be within a certain band or range. As long as the exchange rates remain in your predetermined range, you can effectively hedge currency risk by getting a favorable forward rate. This is a perfect plan to help protect against a worst case scenario and also does not require premiums. The flip side is that, if the prices fall below or shoot above your expected range, you may have to shell out a price that is actually more unfavorable than even the worst case scenario.

Risk Reversal

This hedging currency strategy provides protection against losses in the complete sense of the word. Unfortunately, this strategy limits participation in a favorable market with a cap and sometimes has rates that are worse than the actual forward rates being quoted in the market. Once again, the benefits are that you do not have to pay premiums, you are completely protected against the worst possible scenario and you have the option to restructure your risk reversal at anytime.

Kick Into Forward

Last but not the least, this hedging strategy gives hedging protection for downside risk and conditional participation for upside price movements. While you benefit up to the kick-in level with no initial premiums, full hedging cover and restructuring facility, you are in for a worse off rate if the kick-in level is actually reached.

Companies around the world have long used financial instruments like futures contracts and currency swaps and hedged their currency exposure. But now, as debt markets around the world open to foreign borrowers, a growing number of firms are using bonds for hedging due to improving local economies and accessibility to more borrowers. Hedging is a very important step in financial planning and if done well, serves well in the long run financial management.

Automated Forex Trading Software

The foreign exchange market originated in the Imperial era and was significantly modernized in the post World War 2 era, with its modern conception being largely based upon the stock exchanges and money markets. The Forex market, which is sometimes also known as a currency trading was basically set up in order to help people and companies to convert one currency into another. Just like stock markets, people also trade for profit in the stock exchanges. The mechanism to obtain profit is simple. A United States trader can invest $50 into the Euro of the same value. When the Euro apprises the US trader can immediately convert the Euros into dollars which would be $50 plus something. The only difference in automated Forex trading systems is that this transaction is totally automated.

About Automated Trading Software

There are several Forex trading strategies, that can be implemented by people to obtain profit. However, the Forex market is a huge one with almost all national currencies being traded on the market. The market is basically twofold, with brokers and investors being the two folds. The automated Forex trading systems are basically programs that can be installed on your computers, that can trade currencies automatically, without human supervision.

The working of an Forex trading software is simple, the software scans the market for low-priced currencies and purchases and then sells them into high-priced currencies. Of course, the program is designed in such a manner that it ensures a profit for the investor. There are several different strategies that you can implement with the help of the automated Forex trading strategies, such as arbitrage trading or day trading strategies. Some features of the automated Forex trading software are as follows:

1. Automated trading software gives updates regarding potential currency pairing, such as USD and Euro. Usually the trader already owns some USDs or Euros from earlier trades. In such cases, the price difference can be profited. In some cases, the program can also automatically purchase or sell the currencies without human supervision.

2. Often there is a chance to have an arbitrage trade, i.e., purchase at lower price, and then sell at a higher price simultaneously. This transaction can operate at a much faster rate as the software has much better reflexes than any human investor.

3. Thirdly, the automated Forex day trader also brings updates and advises from across the web and globe at the end of the day which can be easily used by investors.

4. Another operational feature of all Forex software is that they show composite graphs of the projection of several currencies. What more, the graphs are authentic. Such graphs can be used for a comparative study of all the different economies and their currencies.

5. Some Forex day trading systems can be instructed to buy and sell currencies on their own, upon the breach of a particular upper or lower limit of the currency projection.

6. There are countless automated Forex trading systems and software, that can be used by investors. Often brokers also provide the software so that the communication for trading can become faster. There are also several free software packages that can be downloaded.

It must be noted that these software have 'settings', that is, they have to be instructed over what to buy and sell or what should be the total quantity of this purchase and sale. Thus, your own study of the different economies and well thought out anticipations must be a commanding factor of the software. It must be also noted that even the best Forex trading software packages do not have a totally loss-free mechanism. Automated Forex trading is also loss prone, hence be sure that you have a good analysis of the different economies. Apart from that, there are also several scandals and illegal activities regarding such systems and facilities, that have been reported, hence go through some Forex trading software reviews before installing or purchasing one.

Best Forex Automated Trading Robots

For the purpose of ensuring profitable forex trades, one needs to be able to interpret the leading and lagging indicators. Since interpreting signals is not a particularly easy task, especially since leading and lagging indicators tend to produce conflicting results, forex signal systems, both manual and automated, caught on in a big way. Automated forex signal systems, that did not require the presence of the trader to execute trades, took precedence over Mechanical systems, since the latter required the trader to be present, for the purpose of buying and selling, based on the signals received, and thus was not totally effective in removing the human element. Automated forex signal systems also known as forex automatic trading robots, are based on computer programs. These programs determine the currency pair that should be bought or sold at a given point in time by generating standard trading signals. A day trader, who uses the 5 min or 15 min chart for judging the direction of the market, may use the forex automatic day trading robots to make profitable trades.

How are Forex Robot Systems Designed

Forex robot systems are designed by professional forex money managers who use past performance and trends to simulate results that may reflect the actual trading environment. They are based on hindsight which, as we all know, is 20/20. An account may not achieve profits similar to those shown, since past performance is not indicative of future results.

Reviews on Forex Robots

Forex robot reviews are based on the characteristics of the automated forex trading software. The system should be capable of the following, in order to get a good review and be accepted as the best automatic trading robot. Some determining critera are:

Fully Automatic:

The Forex robot system should be fully automatic in order to be successful in eliminating the human element and ensuring round the clock trades without any supervision. It should eliminate the need for forex brokers who were previously required to manage accounts.

Low Account Investment:

People should be able to trade with a low initial trading account since forex robots cannot always eliminate losses because of the very way in which they are designed.

Back Testing Should Yield Results:

This is important since simulations are based on hindsight and past performance.

Inbuilt Loss Protection:

It should have an inbuilt loss protection mechanism in order to ensure that people using the forex robot system do not incur huge losses because of wrong signals.

Constantly Monitored by Experts for Improving Performance:

The performance of the forex robot system should be constantly monitored by experts in order to improve and optimize trades.

The reviews of forex automatic trading robot systems should be useful to traders, brokers and institutional investors. The automated trading software should be of use to traders who are not comfortable trading on their own, but still want to manage their own account. Institutional investors who want to invest across asset classes, in order to reap the benefits of diversification, should find the software useful for investing in the forex market. Brokers should be able to offer automatic forex robots as an additional service to their customers.

Automated Forex Trading

In forex trading, there is a trading program or human experts that make trades for a participant, without him/her actually getting involved. Moreover, with the advent of internet, latest communication technologies, and advanced forex trading systems, taking part in this trading market has become extremely simple for anyone having a computer, an internet connectivity, a forex brokerage account and a good trading program. This system acts as a tool which enables the participant to specify a currency, an asking price and a selling price. Hence, with a small amount and help of a broker, the participant's purchase and sell orders can be executed instantly.

There are generally two categories in forex trading, one is in which the participant has to program their own, or someone else's forex system into a program having programming and automatic trading abilities like WealthLab, or other trading program. These programming skills enable the participant to select parameters and test his/her system performance. The other category which does not require much of trading skills or expertise is automated trading through managed forex, where in a forex trading robot or program executes the trades in place of a human team. Hence, one does not have to do trading all by its own, which not only saves time but also enables the participant to manage multiple accounts from his/her trading platforms, just by constantly monitoring the market.

Benefits

Besides the advantage of trading multiple systems and markets, an automatic forex trading benefits by allowing your trades to be executes at any time of the day or night, irrespective of your presence. Hence, you will not miss on any single transaction, even if you are not present in front of your computer. On an emotional level, it eliminates human emotions and psychology that may affect correct and profitable trading decisions. Also with an automatic system, you will be able to monitor many currency pairs, simultaneously and can follow and execute all of them.

The key feature of an automated forex trading robot is that it is fully programmable and can be customized according to a participant's needs. But even with such a sophisticated and highly efficient trading system, one has to be well acquainted with the basics of the forex trading, methods of fundamental and technical analysis, market indicators, etc. for enjoying consistent and maximum profits.

Determining the Best Forex Trading Software

So what is a forex trading software? Well, these are trading software that help the trader in analysis and trade execution. It is difficult to name the best one because each forex broker has software with different features. Selecting a software is always about personal preference and your technical skills and trading style. The best part about currency trading is you opportunity to make money even if the stock market is low, as there is always a variance in different currency rate.

Types

There are four types of forex trading software and selecting one depends on your need and suitability. Before you zero in on a name, it is first important to understand what type is the trading software available for you. Here are the four types of trading software with the names of best currency trading software for each types.

Web-Based

This type of currency trading is done using a computer with internet connection from any location. Here the trader needs to go online using a user name and password. The main advantage of this type of software is that the user can access it from anywhere in the world and there is no need to download a software. This is a secure trading software, as your information is in an encrypted form and the software provider always has a backup of your data, in case of data loss. Easy-forex and eToro are some of the best software if you wish to carry out online trading.

Computer-Based

This type of currency trading can be done using your local desktop or laptop computer. Though this is convenient for most people, there are a number of risks attached to this type of currency trading, like data loss and computer virus. Make sure you have a good internet connection for fast transfer of data, else it might have a negative impact on your trading. So whenever you use this type of software, always create a backup file, keep the data password protected and make sure your computer has a strong and genuine antivirus software. MetaTrader and VT Trader are good stand-alone forex trading software.

Automated

The introduction of automated forex trading software has made trading easier, faster and less taxing. You do not waste your time understanding and is quite inexpensive compared to other types of software. The convenience of use and implementation, high accuracy, good return for investment and cost should be the important criteria to look for, while deciding the best software for you. These are also known as day trading robots as the trading is done by the software itself with minimum or no help from your end, so it is mostly used by beginners to learn the ropes of the trade. Forex Tracer, Forex Autopilot and Forex Raptor are some highly recommended and best automated forex trading software available in the market.

Managed Account

This is a software for those people who are interested in investing money in forex trading, but do not have the time or interest in trading themselves. Here a trading expert manages your account on your behalf with the help of this software. This is also for those who have tried their hand, but do not have the required knowledge and skills for trading. Some established names of this type of software are CTS Forex, ZuluTrade and dbFX.

Tips for Choosing

Since you are dealing with money, and in a highly competitive market, there are very high chances of loss if you are not cautious enough. Trading means one man's loss is another man's gain. So you don't want to be at the losing end, and want good returns for your investment. These are few tips to help you choose an ideal software platform that is available online:

Tip 1: Never buy software before trying it. Most stock brokers offer a trial version of their software, so try out a few software before you buy one.

Tip 2: Once you have tried a few software, select one that is fast and saves time.

Tip 3: Look for a user-friendly software. You do not want to waste most of your time in understanding the features of the software.

Tip 4: Read the best software reviews and comments online about the software of your interest.

Tip 5: Always check if the software is compatible with your computer system. Otherwise, see if you have the flexibility to upgrade the system.

Tip 6: Check for technical support of the trading software. A good software should also have a good technical support staff, in case of emergency or any glitches.

How often have you come across websites that vouch to make your $1000 to $100000 in four hours? Well the numbers might differ, but the claims are still the same, to make you rich in just a few hours. Don't get fooled by these claims. You are not the only trader in the market, there are thousands of people with the same goal and do not forget, there are Wall Street pros that you are competing against. Whatever you choose as the best forex trading software according to your requirements, the best lesson in currency trading is to keep realistic expectation. Don't expect a miracle by giving in four hours of your time when there a people sitting there trading 24 hours a day. As trading software is an important part of the trading business, always read about the reputation of the software before you invest your money.

Basic Forex Terms Explained

Financial jargon is notoriously difficult to decipher and understand. If you happen to know any economist or financial analyst who can explain them to you, then in most cases their explanation is simply not understandable for lay men who can barely manage to know the difference between stocks and mutual funds and debt and equity. So, if you are like me who gets hopelessly muddled in words like systematic investment fund, collateral, negative equity, reverse mortgages and credit crunch, then you need to get rid of the financial jargon to understand these terms. Carry trade in layman's term means borrowing a currency that has a low interest rate and converting it into a high interest giving currency and then lending it. It is a very risky way of making quick money as the currency market is very fluctuating in nature.

Carry Trade

Basically, carry trade consists of borrowing money at a cheaper rate and investing it somewhere you can earn higher returns from. In a carry trade, the investor borrows money in a low interest rate currency like the Japanese Yen and Swiss Franc and then investing this in higher yield giving assets in a different currency. The higher yield giving currency is often the US dollar but people are also investing in assets such as Icelandic housing bonds. This gives superior returns for investment and this is what has lured many investors into currency carry trade.

For the recovery of the economy due to recession, the US Government and the Federal Reserve has kept the interest rates at a hitherto unheard of low level. According to this policy, small businesses and consumers can get easy funds by taking loans with such an artificially low interest rate, thereby helping the US economy to recover. But investors take advantage of this low interest rate and borrow large sums of money at a low interest rate and invest it in assets outside the country which will yield much higher returns.

Here carry trade is explained with the help of an example. Let us suppose that the interest rate for a commercial loan in United States is 2% and the same loan in Australia has a rate of interest at 5%. An investor simply takes advantage of the difference in the two rates of interest in different economies. An investor will take out a loan with the 2% interest rate in US and exchange the money in Australian dollars. He then proceeds to invest the money in bonds. If there is no market fluctuations this carry trade will earn him a profit of 3% without him having to invest a single penny of his own.

Carry trade might seem like a very attractive way to make a quick buck, but there are many risk factors involved that you should be aware of. The biggest risk factor of course is the uncertainty of exchange rates and if the currency exchange rate works against you. If in the example given above of the Australian dollar weakens or devalues, reducing the assets relative to your borrowing. As a result, the investor will face substantial losses and they still have to pay back the debt in US dollars.

Carry trade can earn an investor very good returns even if they do not have any capital. But it can be risky if the volatility in currency exchange market takes place and it should be best left to those investors who can cope with any potential losses. Now that you know what is carry trade, you can decide for yourself if you have what it takes to risk investing in carry trade or should you stick to more conservative investments.

The Gold Standard

Exact date for the commencement of the gold standard is not known however the 1880-90 period is important. Currencies are valued in terms of a gold equivalent known as the mint parity price (an ounce of gold was worth $ 20.67 in terms of the U.S. dollar over the gold standard period) in gold standard. Each currency is defined in terms of its gold value hence all currencies are linked together in a system of fixed exchange rates. Gold was used as a monetary standard because it is an internationally-recognized homogeneous commodity that is easily storable, portable, and divisible into standardized units, such as ounces. Since gold is costly to produce, it possesses another important attribute governments cannot easily increase its supply.

The Gold Exchange Standard

An international conference at Bretton Woods, New Hampshire, in 1944 at the close of World War II transformed the international monetary system into one based on cooperation and freely convertible currencies. By this each country had to fix the value of its currency in terms of gold. This established the "par" value of each currency. The U.S. $ was the main currency in the system and $1 was equated in value to 1/35 oz. of gold. By this all currencies were linked in a system of fixed exchange rates.

The members were committed to maintaining the value of the currency within +/- 1% of parity. The various central banks were to achieve this goal by buying and selling their currencies (usually against the dollar) on the foreign-exchange market. When a country experienced difficulty maintaining its parity value due to balance of payments disequilibria, it could turn to the International Monetary Fund (IMF), which was created to monitor the provision of short-term loans to countries experiencing temporary balance of payment difficulties.

External and Internal Convertibility

When all holdings of the currency by non-residents are freely exchangeable into any foreign (non- resident) currency at exchange rates within the official margins than that currency is said to be externally convertible. All payments that residents of the country are authorized to make to non-residents may be made in any externally convertible currency that residents can buy in foreign exchange markets. And if there are no restrictions on the ability of a country to use their holdings of domestic currency to acquire any foreign currency and hold it, or transfer it to any nonresident for any purpose, that country's currency is said to be internally convertible. Thus external convertibility is the partial convertibility and total convertibility is the sum of external and internal convertibility.

Externally inconvertible currencies may be of rather limited value to their holder. An exported item from a developing country to the USSR, for example, may be paid for in rubles or the currency of a country that has ratified Article VIII. The proceeds may be used to purchase goods anywhere.

In considering possible import suppliers, therefore, a developing country will have some interest in directing its importers to those countries that will have some interest in directing its importers to those countries whose inconvertible currencies are in large supply. This is, of course, a case of trade discrimination that is condemned by traditional theory. This means that goods are not being purchased from the cheapest source. Recent economic writing has, however, reopened the question in view of the continued existence of inconvertible currencies. Where it is profitable on the export side to trade with countries maintaining inconvertible currencies, and the government wishes to encourage imports from those countries to offset its credit balances, it will utilize its exchange distribution mechanism to limit the availability of convertible exchange where there are alternative suppliers of the same type of goods in inconvertible currency countries.

Currency Convertibility

An international monetary system has been in existence since monies have been traded, its analysis have been traditionally started from the late 19th century when the gold standard began.

Current Account Convertibility

Current account is defined as including the value of trade in merchandise, services, investment, income and unilateral transfers. Being essential to the development of multilateral trade, three approaches to current account convertibility has been adapted by developing countries. These are the pre-announcement, by-product, and front-loading approaches. Each approach is distinguished by the importance it attaches to convertibility relative to other economic objectives.

Capital Account Convertibility

Capital account includes transactions of financial assets. Its convertibility refers to the freedom to convert local financial assets into foreign assets in any form and vice versa at market-determined rates of exchange.

Capital controls normally restrict or prohibit cross-border movement of capital. Thus, controls on capital movements include prohibitions: need for prior approval; authorization and notification; multiple currency practices; discriminatory taxes; and reserve requirements or interest penalties imposed by the authorities that regulate the conclusion or execution of transactions. The coverage of the regulations would apply to receipts as well as payments and to actions initiated by non-residents and residents.

Forex, Currency Trade and Currency Hedging

In the Forex or currency market, international currency of nations is traded (currency pairs). For example, 1 Euro can be traded (exchanged) for 1.4847 USD or 1 USD can be exchanged for 44.2693346 INR (Indian Rupee).

The lesser the rate of exchange and conversion during purchase the better, and more the currency exchange rate during sale, the better, is the key principle for currency and Forex markets. In such cases the currency through which the trade is being conducted is known as the base currency (in this case the USD) and the quote currency is the one into which the base currency has been invested. There are two key ways to make money in the Forex market:

- Invest into the quote currency and wait for it to appreciate and then reconvert into the base currency.
- Wait for the base currency to depreciate and then covert.

Hence investors aim at investing in situations such as 1 USD = 44 INR and sell at situations where the value (not the exchange rate) of the quoted currency rises to 50 INR. The 50 INR that are owned by the trader are then converted into some other currency and then again into USD so that the final sum that the trader receives is more than 1 USD, say 3 USD. It is however, more common for investors to pair the currency. The key is to keep in mind three things, namely, the exchange rates, the appreciation and depreciation of currencies and lastly, the observation of quote currency from the point of view of the base currency. The principle objective of the entire trade is to have more units of the base currency than the quote currency.

Now when it comes to creating a hedge in the currency and Forex market, the risks that have to be hedged include, the depreciation of the quote currency, the appreciation of base currency and any sudden change in the exchange rates. Now appreciation of base currency cannot be hedged, especially if it's your homeland's currency. The remaining two risk factors, on the other hand, can be hedged.

Foreign Currency Hedging

As we have discussed, the basic principle behind currency hedging is to exchange the currency while the rate of exchange is favorable, and then make the investment with currency that is native to the country of origin. This approach is adopted to safeguard the investor against fluctuation in currency exchange rate, and thereby preventing a monetary loss. What basically happens is that, your incomes and expenditures do not get affected by any wayward exchange rate or interest rate fluctuations. If a trader is long on a particular currency, he will protect his downside exposure by hedging it with a perfectly offsetting short position in another market. If you're still confused, the following strategies will make the concept clearer to you.

Foreign Currency Hedging Strategies

You may have guessed that there are various internal and external ways of hedging foreign trade risks. The internal ways are as follows:

Leading and Lagging Income and Expenditures:

A trader can lead (pay in advance) or lag (pay late) his foreign currency payments, depending on whether he expects the foreign currency to appreciate or depreciate, in the near future. The idea is that a foreign currency depreciation (home currency appreciation) translates into lower receipts and higher payments, respectively.

Netting Receipts and Payments:

The idea of netting involves matching (or clubbing) the receipts and payments in a currency, so that any losses in receipts are compensated by the gains in payments and vice versa.

Though there are several other internal strategies available to an investor, the ones mentioned above are the ones prominently used. The external strategies are more popular though, as they offer a broader scope than the internal ones. There is a limit to the amount of risk that can be hedged by the internal strategies, which the following external strategies do not possess.

Forward Contracts

This is by far the most popular means of foreign currency hedging in the world of finance, today. Forward contracts are contracts that lock in a fixed exchange rate, for the receipts and payments. This rate is usually the market determined forward exchange rate. What forward contracts do is offer stability to the receipts and payments. Both parties (the receiver and the payer) know exactly how much needs to be paid or received and the ongoing exchange rate on the date of the transaction hardly matters. This limits the losses but also limits the extra profits that could have been made, had the rate on the transaction settlement date been more favorable than the predetermined forward rate. An equivalent hedging strategy for foreign currency risks in the commodity markets, can be achieved through futures trading.

Currency Swaps

Currency swaps are exchange transaction that take place in real-time, i.e., one thing is exchanged immediately for another, without any lapse or delay in time period. In a currency swap transaction, the principal and payments of a fixed interest contract in one currency, are swapped with the principal and payments of an equal loan in another currency. Sounds difficult but it really isn't so. This is effectively me swapping my one currency fixed payment obligations with you for another currency fixed payment obligations, so that both of us will be dealing in the currency in which we have more faith. Thus reducing our foreign currency risk between ourselves.

Foreign Currency Options

Options are basically derivative instruments that derive their values from the underlying instruments that they represent. Currency options are thus derivatives based on foreign exchange (forex) or currency valuations. Foreign currency options give their holder the right but not the obligation to purchase (call option) or sell (put option) a specific foreign currency. What this does, is that it safeguards the holder's interest. If the market rate of the currency is more favorable than the rate he would receive by exercising his option, he will not exercise it, and vice versa. Come what may, he will definitely be receiving (or paying) an amount that is better than what he would have received (or paid) without this strategy.

Interest Rate Options

Just like all the other option derivatives, the interest rate options give the option holder, the right but not the obligation to purchase or sell a specific interest rate contract. What this does, is that both parties are fully aware of their possible payment and receipts. Also, it is a very good cover against interest rate movements, especially if you're holding a naked position (i.e. uncovered position). This option is however used by interest rate speculators, large banks, etc. It is not generally used as a retail vehicle for foreign currency hedging.

Interest Rate Swaps

Interest rate swaps are basically contracts that allow two parties to swap their particular interest rate exposure with another. This is not a risk neutralizing strategy, just a reallocation of interest rate risk exposure. If someone has floating rate payments and he expects the interest rates to rise substantially in the near future, his greatest worry is how much more will he have to pay. Similarly, for someone with fixed rate receipts, the greatest fear is how much less will he be receiving because of a fall in interest rates. Both the parties (holding opposite views about the future state of interest rates in the market) can then help each others by swapping their contracts with each other and settling the excess receipt or payment. Thus, the first party with the floating obligation will now have a fixed one and the party with the fixed receipts will get a floating receipt.

Spot Contracts

The best way to hedge foreign currency risk is not to take it on the first place. One can protect oneself from adverse exchange rate or interest rate changes by taking on spot contracts. In spot contracts, contract payments and receipts are settled on the day or on T+1 or T+2 settlement terms. This small duration does not allow for massive exchange rate or interest movements and thus safeguards the person from foreign currency risks. This is also a good (almost cost less) strategy.

Foreign currency hedging can also be undertaken by the way of money market hedges. Money market hedge position can use any of the above vehicles to reduce foreign currency risks. They involve borrowing (or lending) money in one currency and converting the payments (or receipts) back to the original currency, to settle contracts without undertaking any risk. Most rates, even those in the future, are fixed forward rates and all interest earned or paid is also on a fixed rate of interest.

Why Hedge with Foreign Currency

To Counter Foreign Exchange Risk Exposure:

When any trading is undertaken in foreign countries, the trading firms are inevitably exposed to exchange rate movements. This risk of the future exchange rate being unfavorable to any firm, leading to losses, is termed as foreign exchange risk exposure and this can be counteracted by foreign exchange hedging.

To Counter Interest Rate Risk Exposure:

When any money is picked up or lent to someone in another foreign country, the interest payments or receipts are subject to the interest rate movements in that country. Substantial movements in interest rates during the term of the contract can lead to abnormal losses to both or either of the parties and this risk is termed as interest rate risk exposure.

To Counter Foreign Investment Valuation Exposure:

Taking positions in foreign stocks or stock markets means getting exposed to speculative risk as well as exchange risk. Both these risks, i.e. risk that the stock price may change adversely and the risk that the exchange rate at the exit position may be adverse, together form foreign investment valuation exposure.

For Hedging Open Speculative Positions:

Any open positions in any market can be counteracted through the foreign currency hedging vehicles.

Who will Hedge with Foreign Currency

Anyone exposed to the risks of operating in various different countries or stock markets needs the aids of foreign currency hedging vehicles. Open positions are highly risky and unsafe. Foreign currency hedging makes all these trades a whole lot safer. So, basically, everyone involved in foreign currency positions, will need strategies to neutralize the extra risks that they are picking up.

The problem with foreign currencies is that their exchange rates are very volatile and subject to change. This volatility can translate into heavy losses if there are adverse exchange rate changes between the date of the transaction and the date of the actual receipt or payment. The easiest way that individual investors can hedge against currency risk is through the use of currency-focused ETFs.

Remember risk tolerance is not the same for all investors and is something that not all of us are willing to take when it comes to investing capital or money. Fear that our current financial situation would be affected due to any predicted or unforeseen event in the future, promotes us to buy insurance, purchase hedge funds, take up fixed annuities, 401(k), IRA and what not. Risk and the feeling of fear would principally get curbed as a result of a hedge. In markets such as the stock markets and the currency or Forex markets, hedges are used to obtain securities and currencies. So basically a hedge is a compound of security, that prevents an investor from falling into a sudden financial loss. It must be noted that though largely effective, a hedge is not completely foolproof. In extreme instances where an entire economy or a substantial section or faction of the economy goes into a depression, the hedge unfortunately, does not remain as effective and useful as before. Now as mentioned above, a common hedge can exist in any kind of market. A currency hedge is of course used to safeguard and secure an investor's interest in the international currency market.

Currency Hedging by Importers

Companies have to hedge foreign exchange exposure, the impact of which can be felt on the income statement and the balance sheet. Foreign exchange exposure refers to financial and economic risk that a company would have to face on account of unfavorable exchange rate movements. The impact of currency fluctuations on the income statement, felt in the form of reduced profits or losses, due to unfavorable currency movements, is known as transactions exposure. The effect of currency fluctuations on the translation of foreign assets and liabilities, of a multinational company for the purpose of accounting in the currency of the parent company, is known as translation exposure.

Exporters and importers face the risk of transactions exposure because the payment received or made is in a foreign currency. For instance, a US based importer may be engaged in importing precision tools from a German exporter. The importer would most likely be required to pay the exporter in Euros. Supposing a consignment of precision tools is to be received by the importer 3 months into the future and in the mean time the dollar depreciates, the importer would be able to purchase fewer Euros with Dollars. In other words, the importer would be forced to pay more for the goods imported. Moreover, since the imported tools become relatively expensive, he may find it difficult to sell the goods in the domestic market. In other words, he incurs a loss on account of foreign exchange exposure. Hence, the need for hedging foreign exchange exposure arises. The following strategies can be used by the importer as a hedge against unfavorable exchange rate movements.

Strategies Importers Apply to Reduce the Risk of Currency Fluctuations

Forwards:

The importer can enter into a forward contract to buy a fixed amount of Euros for a given amount of Dollars. A currency forward contract is an obligation to buy or sell the currency at a predetermined price and at a given date in future, regardless of the price of the asset in the spot market. Assets are traded at the currently prevailing prices in the spot market. The two parties to a forward contract are the long and the short. The long agrees to buy, while the short agrees to sell, the currency at the predetermined price in the future. This arrangement helps eliminate uncertainty, in the amount of payment that has to be made for imports, on account of fluctuating foreign currency. The importer can take a long position in the forward contract and thus eliminate risks.

Futures:

A futures contract was designed in order to overcome the disadvantages of a forward contract. One of the disadvantages, of a forward contract, is that the contract is not standardized. Moreover marking to market feature, that allows for the daily settlement of profits and losses due to fluctuation in currencies, is also not available. In other words, the entire payment has to be made or received, in one go, at some point of time in future. Hence, the chances of default are high. A standardized futures contract is traded in regulated exchanges and marking to market is a must. Hence a futures contract, that allows the importer to pay a fixed price for the Euros that would be purchased at a later date, can help him hedge foreign exchange risks.

Options:

Options, as the name suggests, gives the importer the option of buying the asset or currency at a predetermined price, on or before the expiry of the contract. Forwards and futures allow the importer to eliminate the risk of having to buy Euros by exchanging more Dollars on account of the depreciating dollar. However, if the dollar appreciates, the importer will stand to lose. This is because he would be obligated to buy Euros by exchanging Dollars at the predetermined rate and would be unable to exchange dollars for Euros at the prevailing favorable exchange rate. This disadvantage can be overcome by buying a call option that would give the importer the right to buy the currency at a predetermined rate rather than obligate him to do so. American call options allow the importer to buy the currency at the predetermined contract price on or before the expiry of the contract. European options, on the other hand, allow the importer to buy the currency only on the expiry of the contract.

Swaps:

The importer can enter into a currency swap with a European trader who needs Dollars. In other words, the importer exchanges a fixed amount of Dollars for Euros so that he has the necessary foreign currency to make payments in future. The importer is expected to pay interest, at a fixed or floating rate, on the Euros borrowed while the European trader pays interest on the Dollars to the importer. On the maturity date of the swap, the currencies are exchanged so that the parties have the currency they started out with. These swaps are negotiable for at least 10 years, thus making them a highly flexible strategy for currency hedging by importers.

The type of currency hedging strategy used, will depend on the expectations and needs of the importer. A greater desire for flexibility may propel the importer to opt for swaps and options. In case of forwards and futures, familiarity with the counter party to the contract would determine the strategy. In other words, if the parties to the contract know each other, they would prefer a forward contract that can be customized to suit the needs of the parties. Lack of familiarity would make standardized, exchange traded futures ideal for currency hedging by importers.

E-currency Trading

It is amazing how Internet technology has enhanced and enriched trade via e-commerce web-hosting services. One of the major breakthroughs in trading is E-currency trading. The system or method or application, called and referred to differently in different parts of the world, is believed to be 'tried and tested' by investors. It goes through revision every time an investment is made to prevent the growth of internet hoax. Today, the rostrum is conceivable and successful among industry bigwigs. The forum offers respite to those who firmly disagree that the statistical fact - Futures Trading stands to lose capital within the first year. E-currency trading via internet access has offered such investors a promising alternative.

Understanding the Trade

E-currency is Internet Money that allows the buying and selling of Internet goods and services through internet shopping. Being part of the larger design, the wireless money enables purchases at lightning speed from any of the eCommerce websites. The high level of security makes the purchase safer than those made with the use of credit cards or bank transfers. The trading gurus are rooted to the belief that the demand for e-currency will only grow with dedicated Internet Commerce. It is similar to the disbelief shown two decades ago in a system that would enable access to grocery shopping stores from home with the help of grocery coupons.

How Does the Surreal Currency Work

E-currency trading takes place with the exchange of E-currency. There are hundreds of different e-currencies already in active use. Each currency represents the physical monetary evaluation of a currency or precious metal like a gold investment or in silver jewelry. The currency not only enables wireless payments towards purchases and sales made via Internet marketing, but also helps the owner of the E-currency to benefit when the currency is converted to hard cash. The owner profits from the exchange process via the fluctuation in the determining currency value. This is not much unlike the online currency trading that is commonly carried out via forex.

Strategies To Apply

The rules applicable to E-currency trading are no different to those that apply to futures trading. The value of E-currency is determined, like in the case of other currencies, by the supply and demand. The investment could either be in currency that has the backing of history and performance or opt for ones that are being experimented with. Like in the stock market or forex market, in E-currency trading, too, there is hope in a turn-around. Just like the other established markets, here too, the investor needs to chart every change that affects the online marketing services.

The Advantages

- Leverage to borrow against the present portfolio to buy more e-currency
- Possible portfolio growth between 20% and 40% per month
- Presence of many resources for making money online that update traders on business specific terminology and business resources accessible

The Disadvantages

- Huge learning curve that involves learning unique terminology

- Required investment enough to withstand the 'down' periods

Trading Guidelines

1. E-Currency Trading should ideally be started with an investment of a few hundred dollars. The system should be studied prior to investment and this takes time and research. A small initial investment enables you to build your account block-by-block.
2. E-currency or digital currency like Pay Pal that pays for pay per click advertising is like real money in the real world. When trading in E-currency, the same safety measures need to be applied like the ones you would in the real world.
3. Internet privacy spells internet safety, while availing of wireless internet access.
4. Since the Internet is accessible 24x7, the trading option could be used to start your own Internet business. If the system appeals to you and once the basics are understood, you could look at self-employment with a high speed internet connection.
5. It pays to plan investments and not jump into the fray all at once. Always begin any home based affiliate business in a small, humble way. The same applies to E-currency trade too. There are online resources that help you to understand from big players how much an investment is likely to grow.

Forex Day Trading

Demand and supply are two very important factors that constitute any given economy and market. The forces of demand and supply, their expansion and contraction, their increase and decrease, govern the rise and fall of the prices of a given commodity or financial instrument, or for that matter any possible goods and service that has a given monetary value. This simple principle is applied while trading in the Forex market. In this article, I shall be explaining you about day trading of foreign exchange and its simple mechanism.

Forex Day Trading System

The Forex day trading system is the largest financial market in the world where currencies of all the countries are traded. The currencies are constantly being bought and sold across the Forex market by banks, brokerage firms or organizations and individuals. Due to this, the global markets and investment values increase or decrease as per the movement of the currency. Just like a stock market, the value of global currencies change according to the real world events. A unique feature of the market is that there is no central marketplace to conduct business. Trading is carried out electronically via computer networks between the investors and traders all over the world. It never closes i.e. it is a 24-hour market, so one can trade online anytime.

History of the Forex Day Trading System

By the end of the World War II, the Western nations made the Bretton Woods Agreement that fixed the exchange value of all currencies in terms of the U.S. Dollar. During that time, the U.S. dollar was $35 per ounce and set to the current gold standard. Since the global economy was completely disturbed, the aim of the agreement was to stabilize the world economy and avoid political and social turmoil. It worked well for some time, but later the agreement became outdated and restrictive. Finally, the Bretton Woods Agreement ended in 1971 and the basis of today's currency market was established, with the United States in the lead. The currency market gradually evolved and with the arrival of the Internet, currency trading became much simpler. The continuous practice of depositing U.S. currency in foreign banks exhilarated the Forex market and today the market averages over $3 trillion per day in transactions.

What is Day Trading

In any given market, day trading basically implies trading of currency within a given amount of time. This time span starts with the opening of markets and ends with the close of the market. In case of the Forex market, the concept of day trading is, however, governed by the different time zones. For example, if a Chinese person is trading in the United States Dollars and Euros, his day trading time starts during the evening. In this type of day trading, there are some brokers and institutes that operate round the clock (again with the exception of weekends).

Forex Day Trading Strategies

It has been proved that as a result of substantial growth in the international trade, Forex markets have started booming and many people have started trading in the market to churn out profit. The following are some very simple tips that you can follow.

Trend Following:

The simplest of all Forex strategies is trend following. In such a policy, the investor uses his own intuition to purchase a rising instrument (in this case a currency), and sell it before the fall of the trend. Another situation where the investor can sell the currency is known as a short sell, where a falling currency can be sold before it reaches a point equivalent to initial investment.

Constrain Investing:

Constrain investing is very similar to the trend following. However in such a case, an investor relies solely on a short sell. Here, a constantly rising currency is sold as soon as it crosses a point that is equivalent to investment and same goes for a sale of falling currency.

Range Trading:

There are some trends that rise quickly instantly as soon as they fall or vice versa. The investor can thus invest in a falling rate and sell the same as soon as it rises. This policy can be a bit risky and one has to make a careful analysis of the rising and falling trends.

Scalping:

The fastest and the most difficult strategy is that of scalping. During scalping, a person buys a currency and sells it instantly, almost within a few minutes or seconds. There are basically two drawbacks of this process. Firstly, the amount of purchased units should be large and moreover, it requires a larger initial investment. On the other hand, there is a great risk of the currency remaining stable for a long time.

However, before you take up any kind of trading, it is always advisable to get to know some trading strategies revealed and also some of the principles of economics. I would also recommend you to go through day trading rules, and practice some ghost trading with the help of Forex training.

Conventional Forex Strategies

There are some strategies of Forex market trading that been successfully tried and tested by traders in the past. The simple principle, that is applicable goes as follows.

The basic code that traders follow is, 'buy low, sell high'. Confused? Here's an explanation. Suppose that you buy foreign currency at a price X. Due to the economic conditions, the market value of that currency drastically shoots in an upward direction. In such a situation, you will be able to sell that currency for a price, Y, which is of course, greater than X. The difference is your profit and the investment is the initial low price X. The key to become successful is to understand the rise and fall in the trend of the currency, that you are dealing in. A severe drawback in such cases that there is a high risk of the trend falling down and people losing money in the process. Since the Forex market is an international market, a trend that enters falling cycle, takes time to recover and the trader might end up losing a lot of money or the liquidity (in case if he decides to stay put). The Forex scalping techniques, are preferred in almost any business model or market, as the main emphasis is given on short term buys and sells. Thus, the risk of any dicey trend crashing down is eliminated.

Forex Scalping Strategy

There are two basic types of trading policies that can be followed, namely the long term and short term. The long term policy involves observation and investing for a longer time period, and selling the currency when the trend reaches the pinnacle. As opposed this long term policy, traders also often take up the short term policy that is nicknamed as scalping. While implementing this scalping policy, traders emphasize upon the smallest possible fluctuations and deviations in the market. A small rise or fall is used to make profit when a trader is in a scalping mode. The only drawback of scalping is that the trader has to keep a tab on a large number of transactions at the same time.

The greater the number of transactions, the greater is the profit. The simplest mechanism that is followed in such a case is to buy at rise and sell before fall. The difference between the buy and sell price can be also as low as 50+ pip (also known as points or percentage in point). There have also been cases where the people have purchased and sold at an almost same cost, in order to avoid losses. Market opening cost, closing cost and highest, lowest levels, are the Forex scalping indicators, that are used by investors. Often investors also keep their eyes open for economic news of the currency that they are dealing in as news tends to fluctuate the trends. There are several different Forex scalping methods such as following the trend of a particular set of economies, such as the BRIC economies or only European capitalist economies, or even only North American economies, etc.

On the whole, Forex scalping is not at all an easy, and it involves some serious trend analysis. Some investors are under the false impression that people trading with the help of scalping get lucky and does not have to undertake much of a risk. This is not exactly true as people using this strategy need to put in equally hard efforts in analyzing a large number of trends.

Unlike a stock exchange, a Forex market deals in different currencies and their exchange rates. This market principally came into being to facilitate international trade. For example trade between Great Britain and USA at a point of time was done in USD and Pounds. The transaction here, went through a currency transfer that is a Pound was converted into some Dollars.

The Forex market today is a dematerialized market where all currency trade is carried out though the Internet accounts of the brokers, sub brokers and investors. Now a Forex investor who is based in the United States who possesses

USD will invest some amount in the European Euro, let's say $10. Upon better economic performance, the international value of the Euro will rise. In such a situation, the investor can re-convert the currency into USD again. However, now as a result of the rise in the value of the Euro, it will get converted into say $12 to $13. This is exactly how one makes profit on the Forex market. There are several different strategies that can be used to make a very hefty profit in the market.

Some Forex Secrets Revealed

Here are a few Forex trading tips or secrets which you can use.

- Learn the art of investing in rising currencies. There is nothing known as 'luck', when you deal in Forex. The purchase must be made just before the price rises and sale must be made just before it begins to fall. This will ensure a healthy profit margin.
- Secondly one must be able to make an arbitrage trading. An arbitrage is purchasing at a lower price and simultaneously selling at a higher price. This will ensure that the profit margin is maximum.
- Apart from arbitrage, it is also essential to ensure that you sell just before the fall. That is if you sell too early you will make a profit. However, you will lose the chance of making a healthy profit. To know the exact 'fall' point or the point of satiety, you will have to take up a deep study of the economies in which you are dealing with. Day-to-day events tend to affect this value differentiation.
- You can also take up some related currency tools such as currency options trading or options agreement.
- Some Forex traders keep on trading with a pair of currencies or multiple pair currencies. Such trading is quite convenient in the beginning phases. It is often considered to be the best among all Forex trading strategies for beginners.

- In some cases, the investors deal in a small set of currency; and buy or sell if the currencies tend to breach some or the other barrier that they have set. This is among the best day trading strategies and it ensures a small profit margin.

Overall, Forex trading involves studying the economies and buying and selling the right currency at the right time.

A person who is new to Forex trading, may find it very difficult to understand the various technical jargon or even to analyze the statistics, which are used by the old traders, investment companies, banks or hedge funds to arrive at their investment decisions. But it's not just the statistics, which form the basis of their investments, there are a number of well tested foreign exchange strategies too, which are used by all these parties, to make sound and profitable investment decisions. Any new trader, who is still learning the ropes of the foreign exchange market, can make immediate profits by using these strategies. Here are a few forex strategies that are easy enough for a freshman to follow.

Before learning about the different forex strategies that work, there is one thing that a new trader should know - a Forex strategy is considered useful and effective provided it involves the below given four very important things.

- Appropriate time to enter the market
- Appropriate time to exit the market
- Use stop loss tool effectively and determine where to set the stop loss
- Make profits

Given here are some Forex strategies which effectively make use of all four of these criteria.

Scalping Strategy

Mentioning this once again is worth it. While following the scalping trading strategy, a trader makes numerous trades in a single day, sometimes even hundred. But, he does not hold on to them for long, instead he exits from them if he feels that the market is not responding favorably. In order to make profits by using this strategy, a trader has to make sure that he buys a currency pair at the bid price, and later sells it off for a profit when it gains a bit. The most important thing that the trader should keep in mind while using this strategy is to exit at the right time. A forex scalper has to assess the market situation constantly by studying and making use of the one minute, five minute, as well as the hourly charts.

Margin Account

An effective forex strategy that any trader, especially, a beginner, should learn is to use his money cautiously. One of the ways to protect the money available from getting wasted in bad investments, is to maintain a margin account. A margin account is an account in which the broker lends money to the trader, in return for an interest amount. By maintaining this account a new trader, who may not have enough cash initially, will get some additional dollars to invest and make profits with.

Invest in Currency Pairs

Invest in such currency pairs, which almost always move in two different directions, as far as trading is concerned. For this the trader will have to study the various data, including charts, that are available for the previous year. A trader will have to identify two currency pairs which move in opposite directions so that if one pair goes down and makes losses, it can be covered up by the other pair that will be going up and making profits. This helps in minimizing risks to a great extent.

Like the ones mentioned above, there are many other foreign exchange strategies that work. Another effective strategy is swing trading, in which a trade is held for up to three days. In swing trading, the currency options are sold or bought when they are at the end or near the upward or the downward swing in the market. Thus, to make profits from this or for that matter, any other forex strategy, a trader should follow an appropriate entry and exit policy.

There are thousands of economies and central banks all over the world, that influence the exchange rate between the currencies. This exchange rate is basically established by central banks, such as the Federal Reserve System of the United States of America. The Forex is basically an abbreviation of the term Foreign Exchange. Just as the rise and fall in the stock market can be used as a means of trade, the differences in the exchange rate of the two currencies is used in order to trade and reap the financial benefit of the exchange rate.

The rate of exchange of currencies changes every day. For example, one day, the Euro might be equal to 1.45 United States Dollars, and the very next day, it might change to 1.30 (it must be noted that these figures are just random examples and are not actual). This difference in the currencies that occurs across the world is used as a subject of trade by many individuals and organizations. There are many individuals who, just like the investors of share markets, make use of the difference in values. At the same time, there are many banks, finance institutes, and people involved in the import and export trade, who make use of the foreign exchange market to either make money or save money.

The key advice that you should remember while undertaking Forex trading is "sell before it falls, and buy before it rises". If you are planning upon trading and investing in the Forex exchange market, then it is extremely important to get the right Forex trading education. You might as well try out the Forex trading course that is available on the Internet, which will give you a brief idea about the process that is involved in Forex trading. It is also important that you arm yourself with the good knowledge of Macroeconomic theories. It must be noted that the changes in the Forex market are heavily governed by the Laws of Demand and Supply. Thus, it is necessary to grasp all the essential economic theories.

You will find that there are many different sources that will give you extensive Forex trading tips. However, the best trick to really get the grasp of the Forex market is to have a look at the economies that you wish to trade in. It is best that you stick to a specific pair of currencies like USD and Euro or USD and Yen, or even Euro and Rupee. The best way to keep a tab on the behavior of such economies is to take into consideration trends in these economies, by studying the changes in the prices of the recent past or studying the annual GDP and National Income.

There are also other economic indicators, such as prices of gold and silver or the prices of oil, that you can use to predict and forecast the increase and decrease in the currency exchange rate. You may also observe the seasonal rise in the rates of exchange and also observe the upward and downward projections. The best strategy is to patiently observe growth and sell before the economy starts going into a downward projection.

The Forex trading strategy is another crucial point that you need to follow. For example, select just a handful of national economies and specialize in their observations. For example, you can trade with only Asian economies or only Capitalist economies. After a few month's time, you can and should become an expert in trading with these economies.

There are numerous advantages of Forex trading. The biggest advantage is that you can make a considerable amount of money by just sitting at home and operating a Forex trading account. You will also notice that there are numerable sources that will give you advice. But let me just tell a very nice statement that my economics teacher would recite from time to time. "Want Advice? Ask your knowledge, experience and sense, for advice. They don't have time for nonsense, neither do you and I".

Though forex trading has many advantages over other types of financial instrument trading, it does involve some potential risks and pitfalls. However, knowing some of the best forex trading secrets can give an investor an edge while planning forex investment strategies. Also, being aware of the forex trading pitfalls and the latest technology, one will be having the actual tools required in the market to get most returns for initial investment that too with least risks. So, let us have a look at some forex trading strategies and secrets, which will surely be helpful to all fresh investors.

- The foremost forex trading secret is to know the basics of forex thoroughly, as it will give you a general idea about the trading system.
- Trade in a system, that has consistently proven to be profitable and has an acceptable drawdown. Such a system would have been backtested and also traded in a period of time to testify that it is profitable. Try getting the details of the float, risk management and examples of exact trades with such results.
- While learning the system, be very clear about the system rules and in case of doubts or queries, consult the author of the system or refer to the support forum. Once you know the rules, first trade on a demo account to check whether you can follow the system well or not.
- Apply good money management rules to make sure you can survive and thrive well, in case of any drawdowns.
- Select a system that fits best with your daily routine, for instance some forex trade systems take complete 1 hour daily to trade, like 15 minutes four times a day on average. Hence, also check whether the number of times that system trades, is suitable to you or not.
- Trade patiently and properly, don't over trade, as at times there are no trades for a day and one has to wait till the next day. Also, avoid revenge trading by trading larger trade sizes, in case you had losses in your previous trades.

- It's very important to monitor your progress to know how your system is performing over time, both in terms of returns and drawdowns, and errors that you made while trading.
- If you're deciding to trade with forex signals, automated forex, or managed forex, do your diligence to ensure that the company is authentic and ethical and can provide you samples of their results, having details of the float, risk management and exact trades which achieved those results.

I hope these secrets will be beneficial to all those who want to become profitable traders, without investing much of time and efforts. However, the basic forex trading secret is to learn and practice a good trading strategy well and trade with the trend, by following the strategy rules for unlimited profits.

Forex Trading Strategies for Beginners

Forex trading strategies are in demand as more and more investors are choosing to trade in currencies. However, not all of them are shifting their bases from stock trading and have hardly any information about what energizes or depresses a market, in general. Even knowing about these things won't help the old hands from the stock market that much as currency trading is a completely different ball game. However, within depth study of the trends in and the patterns of the forex trading market, not getting carried away because of the greed and lot of patience anyone, experienced or a beginner, can make reasonable profits by trading in currency.

Everyone is familiar with buying things and paying for them with money. In a nutshell foreign currency trading basics can be explained as, while currency trading, one pays to buy other undervalued currency and when the conditions are favorable, sells the purchased one to buy yet another currency. This market works on the same principle of economics that is applicable to every trade under the sky - that of supply and demand. In this market there is no respite and rest as Forex trading continues 24 hours a day. This is a very volatile market and unless you're on your toes to jump to capitalize the opportunity or duck under the blow, you are fated to be doomed. The first of all foreign currency trading tips for beginners is that don't get in this market without studying how Forex works and what can affect the Forex market, and if you do, make sure that you have a knowledgeable mentor or a broker to guide you in implementing these trading strategies.

The paid as well as free strategies can be classified as simple, complex or advance. However, the goal of every strategy devised must be that of protecting investments and making profit. The following are some of the Forex trading strategies for beginners:

Moving the Simple Average (MSA) Strategy:

The different variants of this strategy concentrates on averaging the values of the currency, under the consideration, over a certain period of time as an aid to make the purchase of a currency. A variant of this, simple Forex trading system of moving averages considers each and every value of currency in that period as important. On the other hand, recent values or the values of the currency that are registered for the middle part of the time period under study are also considered by certain strategies.

Strategy of Hedging:

You can never know when the prices of certain currencies will start falling. Hedging is essential for the most advanced trader and the ripest new beginner. This fact makes the decision of holding Forex a considerable risk. Through this strategy the investors sells when a time period expires. When the prices of the currency that you are holding on to are falling, this surely saves the rugs being pulled from under your feet.

Strategy of Buying on Margin:

If you are a valuable and trusted customer, your broker may decide to extend credit to you to make the purchases. If you are successful you can keep the profit, however, if you lose you have to return the credited amount with interest. To achieve profit use of these trading strategies is not recommended, because, it needs a lot of fast and light footwork to trade the market which a beginner certainly is short of. So, sticking to some easy Forex trading strategies can prove profitable.

You can't learn to swim unless you jump into the water. A beginner wanting to trade in currency market is up against this fact and has to overcome this hurdle. It is essential, along with using the above strategies that one must use automated Forex trading software for online trading. These are a great help in analyzing what is happening in global markets, and what trends are swirling the prices of the currencies. One must, after deciding to trade in this market, to pick a broker or a firm that has holds the membership of the National Futures Association. It is important that your broker gives you access to Forex trading software that allows you to conduct mock trading. This way you can learn a lot by comparing your mock trade with that of the real market.

Technical Analysis

Technical analysis involves studying charts and graphs and comparing past trends and repetitive patterns with the present fluctuations in order to predict the direction of currency movements. Charts used in technical analysis are as follows:

Types of Charts

1. **Line Chart:** A line chart connects the opening price and the closing price with a line.
2. **Bar Chart:** A bar chart gives the opening price, the closing price, the highest price and the lowest price with the help of a vertical bar that shows the range of the currency for a given time period.
3. **Candlestick Chart:** In addition to providing the information that can be obtained from the bar chart, a candlestick chart shows the range between the opening and the closing value for the day, by representing it in the form of a vertical bar. In case the closing value is less than the opening value, the bar is colored.

Chart Indicators

Bollinger Bands:

Bollinger bands are used to measure the volatility of the market. When the market is very volatile the bands expand. When the market is less volatile the bands contract. The currency values always tend to revert to the middle and this is the principal behind the Bollinger bounce. When the market is about to break out, a Bollinger squeeze is observed. A market is said to break out when the currency shifts from the narrow band within which it has been trading for some time.

Relative Strength Index:

Relative Strength Index (RSI) is used to determine whether the market is overbought or oversold. On a scale of 0 to 100, any value below 20 would mean that the market is oversold; while a value above 80 would indicate an overbought market.

Chart Time Frames

Depending on whether one is a day trader, a short term trader or a long term trader, one can use the 5 min/15 min chart, the 1hr chart or the 4hr chart, respectively.

Placing Orders

Just as in the case of stocks, the trader can place a market order, a limit order or a stop loss order in case of forex trading. In addition to these if a trader knows that a breakout is likely but is unsure about the direction of movement of the currency, he can place an OCO (one order cancels the other order) which would result in either buying or selling at a certain price depending on currency movement.

Forex trading can be a rewarding experience for a trader who knows how to use the tools and benefit from the trading platform provided to him by his online broker.

Calculate Your Risk Tolerance

As forex trading involves high risk, it is important to decide the kind of risk one will be able to tolerate and be comfortable with. The trading size can be calculated before making the investment and it is based on the risk tolerance and profit or loss targets. In forex trading, some currencies are more volatile than others and the more conservative traders follow money and risk management rules strictly, in order to avoid losses.

Follow the Trend

The current market trends give a good idea for all good forex trading systems. The investor should have a cognizance of moving averages and the government policies, in order to identify and follow trends. It is necessary to decide prudently the market you want to invest in. As the trading runs for 24 hours a day, it is not possible to monitor and trade in all the markets at all times. The European and US markets are the most liquid markets, but the profit made solely depends on the trading plan and strategies. Currency markets undergo huge trend changes when the fundamental consensus is extremely bullish or bearish.

Create Your Own Strategy

The most important of all the techniques is to create your own trading strategy. It is also necessary to keep on testing these strategies and making appropriate changes from time to time. Nowadays there is also a provision of demo accounts with the brokers, to test the trading strategy you have formed. If the strategy works, it is better to stick to it for sometime before the trend changes. Only constant research of the market and the changing policies can help an investor to come out with a profitable strategy. It is good to learn from previous mistakes and fine-tune your trading plan and strategy. As the investment and risk taking capability of investors differ by huge margins, there is no common and successful strategy for everyone.

Capital Preservation

It is important to preserve the capital when you trade in the forex market. It is not very prudent to trade more than 10% of your deposit, in a single trade, if you are not that capable of taking the risk. If the total capital is of $100,000, every trade should be limited to $10,000, in order to avoid a one time big loss.

Avoid Over-trading

Without sufficient backup, it is very risky to over-trade in the forex market. In an ideal scenario, you should hold not more than 3 to 5 positions at a time. In case of over-trading, investors generally tend to be out of control and make emotional decisions. Such situations usually occur when there is a change in market.

Before jumping head on into the forex market, an investor should remember that the two biggest emotions in trading are greed and fear. An investment should never be driven by any of these factors, as trading is a mechanical process, not meant for the emotional ones.

Free Forex Trading System

While trading in forex currency trading system, the basic policy of each trader applies is to buy cheap and sell when the rates are high. It's very obvious, but then, you need to know when to buy and when to sell. If you master that trick, although difficult of course, you will be able to gain good profits. The uniqueness of forex trade is that currencies are swapped for one another. There are two kinds of transactions which take place - long position and short position. A long position is one wherein currencies are bought cheap and sold at a higher rate. A short position is one in which currencies are sold at a particular price and the same currencies are bought when the value falls.

There are several companies which deal with forex trade, but then you can't always rely on the companies to give you profits. One of the best free forex trading strategies is to learn the jargon's used in forex trade, it may take some time, but it's always better if you know and understand things. It makes things simpler for you. The basic points which you should always look out for are trends in the international trade market and policies of the central banks of different countries. You need to understand the trends and make advanced guesses and take necessary steps. Just as a practice, you can open an account, and then read charts, place orders for selling and buying virtually, besides you can also make calculations, everything virtually. Moreover, you can also go through financial newspapers to get daily news, besides quotes and analysis form experts. Once you are confident, you can start making transactions yourself.

One of the most important free forex trading tips that you should remember is that even though there are several advantages of forex trading compared to other financial instruments, there are some risks and pitfalls. Once you get a general idea of forex basics and about the trading system, you need to trade in only those systems which have a track record of being profitable. While choosing such a trading system, make sure that you check the recent as well as past trends of that particular currency. Get details and examples of exact trade, risk management and float so that you know the currency fluctuations in the past. Ensure you know the rules of the game, and if you have any doubts, you need to consult a financial firm. You need to manage money well so that in case of a drop in prices, you can still survive.

So there are several free forex trading strategies which you need to use, but the basic point is you need to be well versed in how the market works, so that you can't be taken for a ride.

Major Currency Pairs

Name one market which never closes, has the highest turnover volume in the world with people from all countries in the world participating in its day-to-day working. Yes, you guessed it right. It is the foreign exchange market, which extends its dominion all over the world. The market emerged out of a need for a system to facilitate the exchange of different currencies around the world, for the purpose of trade. Now it is the premier financial market of the world, which reflects the financial dynamics of world trade quite clearly. Every trade here is an exchange between currency pairs of two different countries.

As the famous Hollywood movie 'Wall Street's' tag line says, money never sleeps and in case of the foreign currency exchange market it is literally true. As the Earth revolves around herself, sun rises and falls, the forex markets world over, keeps on opening and closing in order to facilitate uninterrupted currency trade.

About Currency Pairs

Foreign exchange trade or forex trading is all about buying and selling currencies in pairs or rather exchanging one for the other. For buying and selling currencies, one need to have information about how much one of the currencies in the pair is worth in terms of the other. The statement of this relation is made in terms of a currency pair. So a currency pair is the quoting of two currency abbreviations followed by a listing of the value of base currency with reference to the counter currency. The foreign exchange rates are decided by the import and export volumes between two countries.

There is an international code which specifies the nomenclature for stating currency pairs. For example, a quote like EUR / USD 1.23 means that 1 Euro is worth 1.23 USD. Here the base currency is Euro (EUR) and the counter currency is US dollar. Thus, every currency pair is listed in the foreign exchange markets across the world.

Major Currency Pairs of the World

Not surprisingly, the most dominant and strongest, as well as most widely traded currency is the US dollar. It features in all the major pairs of the world listed below. The reason for this is the sheer size of the US economy which makes it the biggest economy in the world. US dollar is the currency that is the preferred reference in most currency trading transactions around the world. It is the dominant reserve currency of the world. Following are the major pairs that have high liquidity and take up the major share of forex transactions.

EUR/USD (Euro - US Dollar)

GBP/USD (Pound Sterling - US Dollar)

USD/JPY (US Dollar - Japanese Yen)

AUD/USD (Australian Dollar - US Dollar)

USD/CAD (US Dollar - Canadian Dollar)

USD/CHF (US Dollar - Swiss Franc)

The values of these major currencies keep fluctuating according to each other, as the trade volumes between two countries keep changing every year. For the latest currency exchange rates, refer to sites that offer live foreign exchange reports. They even have currency converters, which can calculate the value of a currency with reference to another, at the current market value.

These major pairs are naturally associated with countries that are financial superpowers with high volume of trade conducted all over the world. The dynamics of the foreign exchange trade is an interesting subject of study as it can provide you with a pulse of the world economy, along with its rising and falling financial fortunes. As the wave of globalization engulfs most countries around the world, the fates of these major pairs are inextricably intertwined. Make sure that you study the foreign exchange market thoroughly before making an investment in this market which never sleeps!

Some Final Currency Trading Tips

Using Leverage Wisely:

Use of leverage is encouraged in the foreign exchange market since fluctuations in the price of a currency pair are typically fractions of a cent. The maximum leverage that can be employed by a trader is calculated using the following formula:

Maximum Leverage (Margin-Based Leverage) = Value of Transaction / Margin Requirement

For instance, if a person wants to control $100,000 worth of trade, he/she can borrow the sum from the broker by depositing a small initial margin. Say, the margin requirement is 2 percent of the total transaction value, the trader is expected to deposit $2000. Thus, the trader's margin based leverage is 50:1. Using excessive leverage, especially when one is unsure about the direction of the market, can land one in deep trouble. Trading on margin is only advisable for people who have the capability of interpreting forex signals or have reliable automatic forex trading robots.

Placing Stop and Limit Orders:

Placing stop orders is useful from the perspective of limiting losses and taking advantage of the potential upside breakout. Placing a limit order allows people to enter a new position or to exit a current position at the specified or better price. A limit order may never be executed because the market price may quickly surpass the limit before the order can be executed. The term better is relative to the nature of the limit order that is placed. A trader, who would like to sell a currency pair, places a limit sell order at a price above the current market price to book profits; while a trader, who would like to buy, sets a limit price below the current price. In the first case, the sell-stop order should be placed below the current market price to attempt to cap the loss on the position while in the second case a buy-stop order should be placed at a level above the current price. These are useful currency trading strategies.

Using Fundamental and Technical Analysis:

Fundamental and Technical analysis are different, although both are necessary from the perspective of gauging currency movements. The former tries to determine fluctuations in the price of the currency by assessing factors that have a direct bearing on the value of the currency; while the latter relies on charts and graphs to effectively compare past trends and repetitive patterns to predict fluctuations in value. The charts, that are used in technical analysis, are Line Charts, Bar Charts and Candlestick Charts.

Line charts connect the opening and the closing price with a line while bar charts use vertical bars to indicate the range of the currency for a given time period. Candlestick charts give the opening price, the closing price, the highest price and the lowest price with the help of a vertical bar. If the closing price is less than the opening price, the vertical bar is colored.

Understanding Chart Indicators: Understanding leading and lagging indicators is critical from the perspective of being able to spot changes that may occur in the movement of currency pairs. These are important currency trading basics.

Leading indicators help a trader spot a change where the previous trend has run its course and the price is ready to change direction again. Lagging indicators provide an indication of the possible changes in trend once the change is clearly visible. The latter is meant to encourage people to move with the herd while the former is useful for a trader who is adept at spotting reversals before they occur.

Although, leading indicators seem like a potential gold mine, they have the tendency of misleading or giving wrong signals. Lagging indicators, on the other hand, rarely mislead. However, the downside is that a person may lose the opportunity to make a huge kill and may end up with a smaller chunk. The most common leading and lagging indicators are Oscillators and Momentum indicators respectively.

Stochastic, Parabolic Stop and Reversal (SAR) and Relative Strength Index (RSI) are examples of oscillators that used to determine overbought and oversold market conditions. For instance, in the case of Relative Strength Index (RSI), on a scale of 0 to 100, a value below 20 indicates an oversold market while a value above 80 indicates an overbought market. If a chart has been indicating oversold (or overbought) conditions, for a certain length of time, one can expect an increase (or decrease) in the price of the currency pair in future. The problem with the aforementioned leading indicators, is that they may provide conflicting signals. In such a situation it would be best to ignore the signal.

Momentum indicators are lagging indicators that generally give the right signal at the expense of delayed entry. People have to choose between leading and lagging indicators since the signals are generally conflicting.

Forex Robots:

Forex trading requires the ability to interpret a number of chart indicators needed for ensuring profitable forex trade. There are numerous forex signal systems that have been designed by professional money managers. These systems have been designed using past performance and trends to simulate results that may reflect the actual trading environment. Both mechanical and automated forex currency trading systems are available in the market. The latter does not require the presence of a trader in order to execute trades while the former provides currency trading tips that are useful for executing trades. Automatic forex trading robots ensure round the clock trades without any supervision and are thus effective in removing the human element from trading. Fully automatic forex trading robots can help one dispense with forex brokers who were previously required to manage accounts. However, one must remember that past performance is not indicative of future results. So, a robot that works well during back testing may not always yield the best results.

A good forex system should be constantly monitored in order to ensure improved and optimized trade. The trading account should require less investment and initially, one should be able to trade with a demo account. Forex robot systems should also have an inbuilt loss protection mechanism since these systems are not foolproof. These robots can be used by traders, brokers and institutional investors.

Advantages of Currency Trading

Increased Liquidity:

As mentioned earlier, forex is the most liquid market in the world. Increased liquidity ensures that the trades gets executed at the desired price.

Ability to Use Leverage:

Increased use of leverage is permitted in the forex market since price fluctuations are typically fractions of a cent. People are allowed to start trading with very little money in their account and are encouraged to control an extensive sum of money in lieu of an initial margin requirement.

Increased Profitability:

The ability to employ leverage results in increased return on investment (ROI). Huge profits with a small up-front investment is one of the benefits of forex trading. Moreover, traders are allowed to split their capital gains to their advantage since regardless of the time of executing the trade, 40 percent of the profits that accrue to the trader get taxed at the short term capital gains rate while the remaining 60 percent is taxed at the lower long-term capital gains rates.

Guaranteed Stops:

People are allowed to place both buy-stop orders and sell-stop orders. The former allows the trader to buy the currency pair at a price that is set above the current market price. The buy-stop order is triggered when the market price touches or exceeds the buy-stop price. People place stop-orders when they would like to trade the potential upside breakout.

Similarly, sell-stop orders can be placed to sell the currency pair at a price that is set lower than the current price. The sell-stop order is triggered when the market price touches or falls below the sell-stop price. These sell-stop orders are placed by traders in order to limit their losses. These are also known as stop-loss orders.

Low/No Processing Fee:

Many brokers do not charge extra fees for opening or closing a trading account, for phone trading, for inactive accounts or for changing stop or limit orders.

No Commissions:

The absence of commission on forex trades is another benefit of currency trading. This is because the spread between the bid/ask price is the compensation for market makers.

The online Forex trading arena is easy and fun to be a part of. It makes your work at home business with a personal computer the most profitable investing opportunity, from any place in the world. Within this day trading forum, you don't need access to stocks or difficult inventory.

The steps to begin trading are as easy as:

1. Open an account with any one recommended or researched broker, with the help of online surveys
2. Pay the sign up fee
3. Invest, after prior consideration of the amount you would like to kick-start with
4. Bag the moolah!

This is in case, you decide to use the services of a professional online broker. If you decide to take advantage of the work at home opportunity alone, , you simply have to:

1. Open an account with any online Forex-trading site
2. Pay up the signing fee
3. Follow the simple instructions provided for purchase and sale of the currencies

4. Rake in the earnings!

In conclusion, the secret of successful trading lies in three basic facts: simple logic, application of some simple economic policies and finally amassing knowledge. These principles, if applied effectively, can easily become the best trading strategies, revealed to the world. Some of these trading strategies have been discussed in the preceding paragraphs and THEY DO WORK! I hope these strategies have been explained in a simple nature and can be used by any person wishing to make money in the vastly lucrative Forex market. Best of luck to you in your endevours.

www.ingramcontent.com/pod-product-compliance
Lightning Source LLC
Chambersburg PA
CBHW070120210526
45170CB00013B/828